FC BAYERN MUNICH

by Jon Marthaler

SportsZone

EUROPE'S BEST
SOCCER CLUBS

An Imprint of Abdo Publishing
abdopublishing.com

abdopublishing.com

Published by Abdo Publishing, a division of ABDO, PO Box 398166, Minneapolis, Minnesota 55439. Copyright © 2018 by Abdo Consulting Group, Inc. International copyrights reserved in all countries. No part of this book may be reproduced in any form without written permission from the publisher. SportsZone™ is a trademark and logo of Abdo Publishing.

Printed in the United States of America, North Mankato, Minnesota
042017
092017

THIS BOOK CONTAINS RECYCLED MATERIALS

Cover Photo: Tobias Hase/picture-alliance/dpa/AP Images, foreground; Schirner Sportfoto/picture-alliance/dpa/AP Images, background
Interior Photos: Matthias Schrader/AP Images, 4; Arne Dedert/picture-alliance/dpa/AP Images, 7; Alastair Grant/AP Images, 9, 10; Peter Kneffel/picture-alliance/dpa/AP Images, 13; ullstein bild/Getty Images, 14, 17; Joch/ullstein bild/Getty Images, 18; Evgenii Iaroshevskii/Shutterstock Images, 20; Markus Schreiber/AP Images, 23; Alexander Hassenstein/picture-alliance/dpa/AP Images, 24; VI Images/Getty Images Sport/Getty Images, 26; AP Images, 28; Werek/picture-alliance/dpa/AP Images, 31; Wolfgang Rattay/AP Images, 32; Frank Augstein/AP Images, 34; Michael Latz/AP Images, 37; Andreas Gebert/picture-alliance/dpa/AP Images, 38; Kerstin Joensson/AP Images, 41; Thomas Eisenhuth/picture-alliance/dpa/AP Images, 43

Editor: Patrick Donnelly
Series Designer: Craig Hinton
Content Consultant: Paul Logothetis, European soccer reporter

Publisher's Cataloging-in-Publication Data

Names: Marthaler, Jon, author.
Title: FC Bayern Munich / by Jon Marthaler.
Description: Minneapolis, MN : Abdo Publishing, 2018. | Series: Europe's best soccer clubs | Includes bibliographical references and index.
Identifiers: LCCN 2016963100 | ISBN 9781532111327 (lib. bdg.) | ISBN 9781680789171 (ebook)
Subjects: LCSH: Soccer--Europe--History--Juvenile literature. | Soccer teams--Europe--History--Juvenile literature. | Soccer--Europe--Records--Juvenile literature. | Football Club Bayern Munich (Soccer team)--Juvenile literature.
Classification: DDC 796.334--dc23
LC record available at http://lccn.loc.gov/2016963100

TABLE OF
CONTENTS

CHAPTER 1

THE TREBLE

In 2013 Football Club (FC) Bayern Munich reached the Champions League final. It was the third time in four years that the club from Munich, Germany, had played for the championship of Europe. But Bayern's fans hadn't had much cause to celebrate in that stretch.

In 2010 the team known as the Reds had fallen to Italy's Inter Milan 2–0 in the final. Bayern's loss in 2012 was even more painful. The Champions League final was held at Bayern's stadium in Munich. The Reds were planning a huge celebration. They had won the title four times but not since 2001. The fans

EUROPEAN SOCCER

The European soccer season is broken down into different levels of competition. It can be confusing to keep track of it all. Here's a handy guide to help you follow the action.

League Play

The 18 best teams in Germany play in the Bundesliga, which debuted in 1963–64. Teams play opponents twice every season for 34 total games. The worst two teams are relegated to the second division. The third-worst team plays the third-best team in the second division, with the winner securing the final Bundesliga spot.

European Play

The top four teams in the Bundesliga qualify for the Champions League, a tournament featuring the best club teams from throughout Europe. The Champions League debuted in 1992. It replaced the European Cup, a similar tournament that had begun in 1955.

The next two teams qualify for the Union of European Football Associations (UEFA) Europa League. The Europa League is Europe's second-tier tournament. It runs in a similar manner to the Champions League but crowns its own winner. The Europa League debuted in 1971 as the UEFA Cup but was renamed in 2009.

Domestic Cups

The best 64 teams in Germany compete in the DFB-Pokal. This includes every team in the Bundesliga and the second division. It also includes the top teams in the third division. The 24 other teams are the best teams from regional leagues. The competition was founded in 1935.

were ready to celebrate. Instead, English opponent Chelsea tied the game late in regulation. Then Chelsea won it on penalty kicks. Bayern's fans and players were crushed.

Bayern players hoist coach Jupp Heynckes in celebration after clinching the Bundesliga title in 2013.

But Bayern bounced back, and a year later the club put together a historic season that made its fans forget about its recent woes. The Reds won the Bundesliga title for the first time in three years. They also made it to the finals of the DFB-Pokal and the Champions League. They were close to winning all three trophies in the same season for the first time.

Champions League Drama

The Bavarians had cruised through the Champions League playoffs again. Bayern finished in first place in its group. The Reds slipped past English foe Arsenal in the Round of 16. In the quarterfinals, Bayern beat mighty Juventus of Italy. This meant that Bayern would play Barcelona in the semifinals. Many people considered Barcelona the best team in the world. But Bayern handled the Spanish giants with ease, winning 4–0 and 3–0 to progress to the final.

It was May 25, 2013. Bayern's opponent for the European championship was Borussia Dortmund. It was the first all-German final in the Champions League or European Cup, as it was known until 1992.

FAST FACT

Bayern is the German word for Bavaria. This is the region of Germany that Munich is in. Many German teams are named after their regions. *Borussia* is the word for Prussia. This explains the names of the Prussian teams Borussia Dortmund and Borussia Mönchengladbach.

Dortmund had won the Bundesliga title the previous two seasons. Bayern had lost five of its previous seven games

Mario Mandžukić chips the ball past two Dortmund defenders and into the net to put Bayern on top in the Champions League final.

against its league rival. The teams had developed a healthy respect for each other. There was no way the Reds would be overconfident again against their rivals from Dortmund.

Dortmund got off to a fast start with several great chances to score early. Bayern goalkeeper Manuel Neuer had to make a handful of big saves to keep the score 0–0. At halftime, the game remained scoreless.

In the 60th minute, Bayern drew first blood. Winger Franck Ribéry slipped the ball through three defenders to forward Arjen Robben. Robben went around the goalkeeper and passed the ball across the goal. His teammate Mario Mandžukić was there to poke the ball into the net.

Eight minutes later, Dortmund tied it. Dante, a Bayern defender, was called for tripping in the penalty area. Dortmund's Ilkay Gundogan beat Neuer from the penalty spot. The score was 1–1.

Robben to the Rescue

As the clock wound down, extra time appeared inevitable. Bayern's fans could feel a repeat of 2012. Losing the title at home was one thing. But losing to Dortmund would be worse. But in the 89th minute, Ribéry and Robben came through again.

Bayern captain Philipp Lahm gets a ride from backup goalkeeper Tom Starke as he shows off the Champions League trophy.

Defender Jerome Boateng lofted a long pass forward. Ribéry controlled it and back-heeled the ball past a defender. Robben ran onto the loose ball and was alone with the goalkeeper. He rolled a shot back across his body and inside the post. It gave Bayern a 2–1 lead. Dortmund did not have enough time to score again. For the fifth time, Bayern was the champion of Europe.

One week later, the Bavarians took on Stuttgart in the final of the DFB-Pokal. Thomas Müller scored in the first half. Mario Gomez scored twice in the second half. Although Stuttgart scored two late goals, Bayern held on for the 3–2 win. It gave the Reds all three trophies that they could win in one season.

Through 2016 Bayern had won the Bundesliga 26 times and the DFB-Pokal 18 times. It had won the Champions League five times. But only in that special 2012–13 season did FC Bayern Munich pull off the treble, winning all three trophies in the same season.

Bayern players celebrate on the balcony of the Munich town hall after winning their historic treble.

 Mia san #Triple
und
IHR SEID WELTKLASSE!

CHAPTER 2

BIRTH OF A SUPERCLUB

The history of soccer in Munich can be traced back to 1897, when a group of players joined a men's gymnastics club. That club also had a men's soccer team. At the time soccer wasn't very popular in Germany. The game came from England, so the German players were still learning to play it well.

However, the game was growing in Germany. A league called the Southern German Football Association had formed. On February 7, 1900, the gymnastics club voted on whether its soccer team should join. The club voted against it.

Eleven soccer players left the meeting in protest. They went to the Gisela Inn in Munich and founded a new soccer-only club. It was called FC Bayern Munich.

The new club was based in the Schwabing district of Munich. Many artists and students also lived in Schwabing. Until World War I (1914–1918), all club members were required to have an educational degree. So Bayern became a club for educated and cultured people, not the working class.

Beginning the Climb

In those early years, Bayern was not very successful. The club won its first Southern German championship in 1926 and its first Germany-wide championship in 1932. The club also won the DFB-Pokal in 1957. It was an unexpected win. Bayern was not a powerhouse. The club did not emerge as a power until the mid-1960s.

Bayern captain Franz Beckenbauer, *right*, meets the captain of Borussia Mönchengladbach before a Bundesliga game in 1965.

The Bundesliga was formed in 1963. Bayern had not done well enough in previous seasons to be part of it at the start. Bayern wasn't yet the superclub it would become. It began in Germany's second division. Soon, however, a group of talented young players led the team to promotion. Bayern joined the Bundesliga in 1965–66.

FAST FACT

Until the Bundesliga was formed in 1963, there was no nationwide German league. The German championship was a playoff between the regional champions.

Bayern players pose with the Bundesliga champions' trophy after winning the league in 1969.

The team had early success in the top division. It won the DFB-Pokal four times in six years, the UEFA Cup-Winners' Cup in 1967, and the Bundesliga in 1969. Winning that much was a new experience for the team. But Bayern was just one of several good teams in Germany.

New Home

In 1972 Bayern moved into Munich's Olympic Stadium. It was built for the 1972 Summer Olympics and was the biggest stadium in Germany. This gave Bayern a financial advantage over its competitors. The Reds were immediately successful at the Olympic Stadium. They won three straight Bundesliga titles from 1972 to 1974. With their new stadium and newfound success, Bayern began its journey to becoming a superclub.

Winning the Bundesliga brought another reward. It gave the Reds an entry into the European Cup. In the 1970s, Bayern was the first team whose European Cup games were shown on German television. This brought them fans from around the country. And the Reds gave the fans reason to cheer. Bayern won the European Cup in 1974, 1975, and 1976.

Bayern struggled in the late 1970s, going five years without a Bundesliga title. Starting with 1979–80, though, the Reds have hardly failed. As of 2017, Bayern Munich had won the German league title in 22 out of 37 seasons. During the same span, the club won 13 DFB-Pokal titles, two Champions League titles, and a UEFA Cup. Bayern has become the superclub of Germany. It is one of the most famous teams in the world.

FAST FACT

UEFA once allowed any team that won three straight European Cups or five overall to keep the cup. Bayern still has the European Cup from 1976. Only five other teams have accomplished this feat.

CHAPTER 3

The Bayern Munich logo recalls the Bavarian coat of arms.

TALENT AND TRADITION

Bayern Munich has had plenty of success on the field. It's also one of the richest clubs in the world. This explains why the best players from other teams often choose to play for Bayern. They want to have the chance to win a Champions League title and become worldwide stars. Dortmund is Bayern's great rival and does well in Europe. But even Dortmund regularly loses its best players to Bayern. This means that fans of other German teams usually root against Bayern.

Rivals

Bayern Munich has always had a rivalry with the other Munich team, 1860 Munich. But 1860 Munich was relegated out of the Bundesliga in 2004. The teams have met in a competitive game just once since then. It was in 2008 in the DFB-Pokal, and Bayern won 1–0.

One of Bayern's more recent rivalries is with Borussia Dortmund. The two teams usually begin the season with the best chance to win the Bundesliga title. Starting in the 1993–94 season, Bayern won 15 of the next 24 league championships. Dortmund won five in that span, and no other club won more than one. Some fans call the matches between the teams *Der Klassiker* ("The Classic," in German). Bayern also has rivalries with VfB Stuttgart and FC Nuremberg, both of which, like Munich, are located in southern Germany.

FAST FACT

The blue and white diamonds in Bayern's logo are based on the Bavarian coat of arms. The diamonds appear in the middle of the coat of arms. This symbolizes the unity of Bavaria.

Play often turns physical when the Reds meet rival
Borussia Dortmund.

Here Come the Reds

The team's red and white primary colors date back to 1906. That
year FC Bayern briefly merged with the Munich Sports Club
(MSC). At the time, the MSC's color was red. So Bayern started
playing in white jerseys and red shorts. Soon people called the
team the "Reds." Since then, Bayern's primary color has been

red, although the team's uniforms have also featured blue and sometimes black, too.

German Traditions

Bayern makes a point of instilling a sense of tradition in its players. All new team members receive a set of lederhosen. These are the leather work shorts that were traditionally worn in Alpine regions of Bavaria. They come complete with suspenders. Players wear them to the annual Oktoberfest celebration in Munich.

FAST FACT

Since 2005 Bayern has shared the Allianz Arena with its crosstown rivals. On days when Bayern Munich plays there, the stadium's outside is lit up with red lights. On 1860 match days, it's lit up with blue lights. Blue is 1860's main color.

Arjen Robben and his family take part in the annual Bayern tradition of attending Oktoberfest in 2016.

CHAPTER 4

STARS OF THE PAST

Bayern Munich's rise to the top of German football started with a slap in the face. Franz Beckenbauer grew up as a fan of 1860 Munich. He planned to join that team after his youth career. But in the late 1950s, during a contentious game in an under-14 tournament, a player from 1860's youth team slapped Beckenbauer in the face.

That incident ended Beckenbauer's desire to play for 1860. He decided to join then-struggling Bayern instead. He convinced his friends Gerd Müller and Sepp Maier to join

Gerd Müller, *right*, heads home a goal in the 1974 European Cup final against Atlético Madrid.

Bayern, too. At the time, nobody could have guessed the impact that one slap would have on both clubs' fortunes.

Beckenbauer is considered by many to be the best German player of all time. Although he was a central defender, or sweeper, Beckenbauer would also go up field and attack the goal. His revolutionary play made him a force for Bayern Munich and the West Germany national team.

The Bayern captain won the Ballon d'Or—or Golden Ball, given each year to the best European club player—in 1972 and 1976. German fans called him *Der Kaiser*, which is German for "The Emperor." He also played in three World Cups for West Germany, finishing no lower than third place and winning the trophy as captain in 1974.

Beckenbauer's friends were no slouches, either. Müller won the Ballon d'Or in 1970. He scored 533 goals in 585 appearances for Bayern. And he was even better for the national team. Müller scored an astonishing 68 goals in 62 games for West Germany. A top scorer would be happy with one goal every two games. Müller averaged a goal almost every time he played. He won the Golden Boot seven times for being the Bundesliga's top scorer.

Maier became a widely praised goalkeeper for both his club and his country. He had such good reflexes that he was known as "the Cat from Anzing," his hometown. He played in four World Cups for West Germany and spent 19 seasons with Bayern Munich.

Together, Beckenbauer, Müller, and Maier won the Bundesliga four times, the DFB-Pokal four times, and the

European Cup three times. Meanwhile, 1860 Munich hasn't won a Bundesliga title since 1966. The club has spent most of that time in the second or third division.

Two More Stars Switch Sides

Beckenbauer didn't just influence Maier and Müller. In 1970 he talked West German national team assistant coach Udo Lattek into coaching Bayern. Lattek had worked with the country's youth teams. He got Paul Breitner and Uli Hoeness, both of whom were set to play for 1860 Munich, to play for Bayern instead.

Breitner was the leader of the club after Beckenbauer left in 1977. He played two separate stints for Bayern. He also played for West Germany's national team. Hoeness scored lots of goals in the 1970s, but a knee injury cut his career short. He had to stop playing at the age of 27. But then he started his career as Bayern's business manager. He oversaw a period of tremendous growth and success for the club.

The team acquired another future superstar in 1974 when it brought in an 18-year-old striker. Karl-Heinz Rummenigge cost Bayern a little less

Sepp Maier was one of the top goalkeepers of his generation.

Paul Breitner, *left*, and Karl-Heinz Rummenigge starred for Bayern in the post-Beckenbauer years.

than $7,000. By 1976 West Germany's national-team coach was describing him as "our best man." He and Breitner—often referred to as "FC Breitnigge"—led Bayern to two Bundesliga titles in the early 1980s. He won the Ballon d'Or in 1980 and 1981. He also won the Golden Boot award in Germany three times. Only Müller scored more goals for Bayern.

FC Hollywood

By the 1990s, Bayern's players were known for being great on the field. But they were also known for fighting with each other off the field. The press nicknamed the team "FC Hollywood" for all the drama surrounding the club.

The best players, and most dramatic offenders, were Lothar Matthäus and Jürgen Klinsmann. Matthäus was an outstanding midfield player who scored many goals off powerful long-range shots. He won the 1991 World Player of the Year award while playing for Inter Milan. Klinsmann was a great striker, known for his aerial goals and for always having a smile on his face.

FAST FACT

In 2016 Carlo Ancelotti became the 20th coach in Bayern history. It was his first time coaching the Reds, but four men have had more than one term as coach. Jupp Heynckes was the coach three different times.

Klinsmann and Matthäus didn't get along. Matthäus was mad that Klinsmann replaced him as German national team captain in 1996. He thought Klinsmann had plotted to get him replaced. The next year, Matthäus bet the team manager that

Klinsmann wouldn't score 15 goals in one season. Klinsmann made certain that Matthäus lost that bet.

Klinsmann's smile disappeared when he talked about management. He once put his foot through an advertising display when he was unhappy about being substituted. Matthäus, too, made himself unpopular. Uli Hoeness, who was then the team's business manager, swore that Matthäus would never work with Bayern again, not even as a groundskeeper.

Bayern has dominated German soccer every decade since the 1980s. The 2000s were particularly great. Bayern won six titles in the first decade of the new millennium. The Reds also finished second twice. They had many great players during this era, but three stand out. Goalkeeper Oliver Kahn and midfielders Mehmet Scholl and Bastian Schweinsteiger all were part of eight teams that won the Bundesliga title. That is a record, even for Bayern, the home of champions.

Lothar Matthäus, left, and Oliver Kahn were key figures of the "FC Hollywood" era.

Kahn started playing for Bayern in 1994 and retired in 2008. He was a favorite of the fans, who made sure he knew it. Once, when the club was going through a particularly bad spell, fans held up a banner that said, "Apart from Olli, you can all leave." He was named the top goalkeeper in the world three times.

For many years, Scholl was the attacking midfielder who provided the offense while Kahn provided the defense. Scholl was particularly known for his amazing free-kick goals. His most famous goal might be a free kick he scored against rival 1860 Munich in February 2003. He launched the shot from more than 30 yards away, beating the goalkeeper into the top left corner of the net. It was the first of his three goals that day. By the time he retired in 2007, Bayern's fans had voted Scholl one of the greatest 11 players in club history.

From 2002 to 2015, Schweinsteiger was the engine that drove the Bayern Munich machine. He controlled games as a midfielder who covered the whole field. His energy and passing skills were key for the Reds to stop the opponents' attacks and start their own. Schweinsteiger could play as a defensive midfielder and still burst forward into the attack. He won eight league titles and the Champions League during his time in Munich.

Mehmet Scholl celebrates a goal in 1998.

CHAPTER 5

MODERN STARS

Today Bayern is a European superclub. In 2016 Bayern became the first club to win four Bundesliga titles in a row. The Reds have enjoyed great European success, too. They won the Champions League in 2013. They were runners-up in 2010 and 2012. And they reached the semifinals in 2014, 2015, and 2016. Barcelona and Real Madrid are the only other teams to have reached the final four in five consecutive years.

Wingers Franck Ribéry and Arjen Robben have been among the club's brightest stars. Both cost Bayern lots of money to bring them to Munich. Because of the team's success it has been able to afford some of the world's best players. Ribéry joined the club in 2007 and was the UEFA Player of the Year in 2013. He plays on the left wing most often and is a dangerous attacker. The Frenchman was one of the club's first big-money purchases. The Reds have gotten their money's worth. Through 2016 Ribéry had helped the team win six Bundesliga titles, five DFB-Pokal titles, and the Champions League.

On the other side, Robben began playing wing for the club in 2009. More than anything, he loves to cut inside and shoot with his left foot. Ribéry, meanwhile, uses his speed and skill with the ball at his feet to blow by defenders. In Ribéry and Robben—sometimes known together as "Robbery"— Bayern effectively has two extra

Robert Lewandowski has been one of Bayern's most prolific scorers since 2014.

strikers playing on the wings. Robben also cost big money. His Champions League-winning goal in 2013 might have been worth it all by itself, in the minds of Bayern's fans.

Superclub Superstars

Polish striker Robert Lewandowski joined Bayern Munich in 2014. In his first three seasons with the Reds he scored more than 100 goals. He's been called the most deadly striker in the world. In September 2015, Lewandowski came on as a halftime substitute in a game against VfL Wolfsburg. He quickly made up for lost time by scoring five goals in nine minutes—an example of his immense scoring talent.

Between the two is striker Thomas Müller. He has the same last name as the great Gerd Müller, and in some ways the two are alike. Like Gerd Müller, Thomas Müller is a prolific scorer despite an unconventional playing style. He is not the fastest, the strongest, or the most gifted player on the field. He is not a great jumper. Some say that he runs like the Tin Man from *The Wizard of Oz*. All he does is score goals—all the time.

Philipp Lahm joined Bayern in 2002 and became one of the top defensive midfielders of his generation. He was the team's

Manuel Neuer makes a save in a 2017 Champions League game against Arsenal.

captain from 2011 until he retired in 2017. He also captained the Germany national team to a World Cup title in 2014.

Backing up all this firepower is goalkeeper Manuel Neuer, who has changed how keepers are expected to play. Not only is he an amazing goalkeeper, but he is athletic enough to play as an extra defender. His speed allows him to rush out of his net and break up attacks. And he has such good skills on the ball that he often takes penalties if Bayern gets into a shootout. Together they have solidified Bayern's status as one of the world's top clubs.

FC BAYERN MUNICH
TEAM FILE

NAME: Football Club Bayern Munich

YEAR FORMED: 1900

WHERE THEY PLAY: Allianz Arena, Munich, Germany

BUNDESLIGA TITLES: 27
(most recent in 2016–17)

DFB-POKAL TITLES: 18
(most recent in 2015–16)

EUROPEAN CUP/CHAMPIONS LEAGUE TITLES: 5
(most recent in 2012–13)

KEY RECORDS

- Most career appearances:
  Oliver Kahn, 632

- Most career goals: Gerd Müller, 525

- Most consecutive Bundesliga victories:
  19, 2013–14

AUTHOR'S DREAM TEAM

GOALKEEPER: Sepp Maier

DEFENSE: Paul Breitner,
Franz Beckenbauer,
Hans-Georg Schwarzenbeck,
Philipp Lahm

MIDFIELD: Lothar Matthäus,
Franck Ribéry, Arjen Robben,
Mehmet Scholl

FORWARDS: Karl-Heinz Rummenigge,
Gerd Müller

TIMELINE

1900

FC Bayern Munich is founded by 11 members of the MTV Munich gymnastics club.

1926

Bayern wins the Southern German Football Championship, its first title.

1932

Bayern wins the German Championship, its only nationwide league title before the Bundesliga was founded in 1963.

1959

Franz Beckenbauer joins the Bayern Munich youth team, at the age of 14.

1969

The Bavarians win the Bundesliga for the first time.

1976

Bayern Munich wins the last of three consecutive European Cups.

1980

Bayern wins the Bundesliga title for the first time in six seasons—still the longest drought since the club's first league title in 1969.

2001

In a penalty shootout against Valencia, Bayern wins the Champions League, its first European title in 25 years.

2013

Bayern wins the Bundesliga, the DFB-Pokal, and the Champions League in the same season.

2016

The Reds win their record fourth consecutive Bundesliga title.

GLOSSARY

extra time

Two 15-minute overtime periods played if the score is tied at the end of 90 minutes plus stoppage time.

forward

Also called a striker, the player who plays nearest the opponent's goal.

free kick

An unguarded kick awarded to a team after a foul.

Golden Boot

An award given to the person who scores the most goals in a league or tournament.

midfielder

A player who stays mostly in the middle third of the field and links the defenders with the forwards.

Oktoberfest

A traditional fall festival in Munich.

penalty area

The box in front of the goal where a penalty kick is awarded if a player is fouled.

penalty kicks

A tie-breaking shootout at the end of games.

sweeper

A defender who plays in the middle of the field and has the freedom to move about the defensive zone rather than stay with an attacker.

winger

A player who plays mostly along the edges, or "wings," of the field.

FOR MORE INFORMATION

BOOKS

Marthaler, Jon. *Soccer Trivia*. Minneapolis, MN: Abdo Publishing, 2016.

McDougall, Chrös. *Best Sport Ever: Soccer*. Minneapolis, MN: Abdo Publishing, 2012.

Monnig, Alex. *The World Cup*. Minneapolis, MN: Abdo Publishing, 2013.

WEBSITES

To learn more about Bayern Munich, visit abdobooklinks.com. These links are routinely monitored and updated to provide the most current information available.

PLACE TO VISIT

ALLIANZ ARENA AND FC BAYERN ERLEBNISWELT
Allianz Arena, Ebene 3
Werner-Heisenberg-Allee 25
80939 München
Phone: (089) 699 31-222
fcbayern.com/erlebniswelt/en

Even when the Reds aren't at home, fans can get the full Bayern Munich experience. The Street of Triumphs is packed with every domestic trophy the club has ever won—and it's a long street. The café is called the Gisela, after the place where Bayern was founded. Stadium tours are available, even on a match day, when the Allianz Arena comes to life. Best of all for fans who don't speak German, the audio guide to the tour is available in English.

INDEX

ABOUT THE AUTHOR

Jon Marthaler has been a freelance sportswriter for more than 10 years. He writes a weekly soccer column for the *Minneapolis Star Tribune*. He lives in St. Paul, Minnesota, with his wife and daughter.